HARDWIRED

The 10 Major Traits of Women Hardwired By Evolution That Can Save the World

The New Science of How
A Woman's Brain
Is Hardwired To Save the World®

Alexia Parks

TheEducationExchange.org
Boulder, CO USA

Books by Alexia Parks

Parkinomics: Eight GREAT Ways to Thrive in the New Economy

Dr Joel's Be Super Fit™ for Life! (Co-Author)

Focus on Success: A 10 Step Mentoring System for Schools

An American GULAG: Secret P.O.W. Camps for Teens

10 Golden Rules That Guide Loving Families (English/Spanish)

10 Golden Rules That Guide Teacher-Mentors*

How Changing Your Name Can Change Your Life

Rapid Evolution: Seven Words That Will Change Your Life Forever!

People Heaters: How to Keep Warm in Winter

How Love Heals (Series)

OM Money Money (ebook)

HARDWIRED: The 10 Major Traits of Women Hardwired By Evolution That Can Save the World -- Copyright © 2012 by Alexia Parks and Joel Rauchwerger.

TheEducationExchange.org, Publisher
303-443-3697 (SAN #253-0872)
973 5th Street, Boulder, CO 80302 (303) 443-3697

"The World Will Be Saved by the Western Woman"
The Dalai Lama

**"The Fastest Way to Change Society is to Mobilize the
Women of The World."**
Charles Malik, former President of the United Nations General Assembly

**"If ever the world sees a time when women shall come together
purely and simply for the benefit of mankind,
it will be a power such as the world has never known."**
Matthew Arnold, 19th Century philosopher

With Special Thanks To

Dr Joel Rauch, M.D. (Rauchwerger) worked with well-known cardiologist and heart surgeon Dr Michael DeBakey, and was on the faculty (1973) at the Baylor College of Medicine, Division of Experimental Biology in the Department of Surgery, Houston, Texas. At age 34, he made a major discovery in the field of Bone Marrow Transplantation.

He was also part of the team of medical doctors who worked on the case of the **"Baby in the Bubble"**, the baby born without an Immune System. This event was turned into a movie: *The Baby in the Bubble*, starring John Travolta.

What makes Dr. Rauch unique is his encyclopedic knowledge of science, medicine, brain function, nutrition, biochemistry and physiology, as well as the fundamentals of basic, good digestion, human psychology, stress management and biofeedback.

Website: http://drlongevity.org

ABOUT THE AUTHOR

Alexia Parks, called "One of 50 people who matter most on the Internet" by *Newsweek Magazine* for her visionary launch of the electronic democracy website, Votelink.com, has enjoyed life at the leading edge of change for more than 30 years.

She has written for the national desk of *The Washington Post*, been a New York City magazine publisher, and served as communications director for a network representing publishers at 100 major daily metropolitan newspapers.

As an innovative entrepreneur, she co-founded the Tarrytown 100, and served as president of Media Syndicate. Currently, she chairs the non-profit TheEducationExchange.org, where she founded a mentor training system for schools called "Focus on Success."

Alexia is also the author of 12 books, including *Parkinomics*, a business and motivational bestseller on *Amazon.com*, and is a Huffington Post blogger. She was the first accredited blogger for the (2007) United Nations Climate Change Conference in Bali. – Website: AlexiaParks.com

Alexia is an in-demand lecturer, inspirational speaker, and educator.

Table of Contents

PART I

Table of Contents
PART II

INTRODUCTION

This is a book for women. It is also a book for men who support the causes women are interested in, or who are simply curious about the 10 special hardwired traits that women possess.

These 10 major traits, hardwired into a woman's brain by Evolutionary Biology, are exactly the opposite of those hardwired in men.

And, they are the very traits that a great leader needs today, in order to successfully manage our complex, volatile world.

The truth is, these 10 important traits of women are needed in leadership roles at all levels of society.

Hardwired, they represent *a major paradigm shift* that once understood, will forever change the way we look at women, politics, and leadership.

In fact, these hardwired differences relate to every single human being on the planet, and every single human endeavor. They show up in the way we respond to relationships, the workplace, to politics, to economics, to the environment, to raising children, to adolescents, to marriage, and about 100 other major topics.

So, if there truly is a need to *"Save the World,"* there needs to be a quantum shift toward women in leadership roles at all levels of society.

This book of powerful insights concludes with one final, BIG insight. And that is how women can step into leadership roles virtually "overnight."

Alexia Parks

A PARADIGM SHIFT

Throughout my whole life I have been concerned with "Save the World" type issues, in all of their forms and varieties. It has been a lifetime journey, a lifetime quest.

My focus of interest has always included a combination of the environment, entrepreneurship, innovative technology, and communications. I've written about these issues in many different books and blogs, as well as created numerous businesses that offered "Save the World" type solutions.

However, the epiphany that I had as I began work on this book, is that it requires a constellation of many fields of human endeavor to address and resolve the many problems of the world, but especially those inequities that women face.

So this book represents a grand synthesis of facts that have been meticulously researched, documented, and pieced together over a 40- year period of scholarship. This grand synthesis, as you will soon discover, forms the basis of a **major paradigm shift** for humankind.

We are making this prediction, based on a quantum leap in our own thinking. It is a groundbreaking discovery made possible by piecing together significant findings from many different fields of research and science, and then applying them to men, women, and society at large.

Our discovery comes from the convergence of many fields including: a knowledge of cultural and physical anthropology, a knowledge of brain function in both men and women, the understanding of the physiology of hormones in both men and women, the psychology of perception in both men and women, and a broad knowledge of cultural studies, world history, and human endeavor.

And, our conclusion is this: That one of the most astonishing discoveries in human history that has been grossly overlooked, until now, is the fact that through the process of evolutionary biology, **a woman's brain has been hardwired for exactly the traits needed today to save the world!**

While this may sound kind of dramatic, you will see by a review of the 10 different hardwired traits of men and women, in the chart found in Part II, that this is true.

In fact, what the chart will show is that the traits hardwired in women are virtually the opposite of those hardwired into men. They are diametrically opposed, and have been so over millions of years.

It isn't that men are better than women, or women are better than men, it's simply that their brains are hardwired differently, to manage *different* tasks.

Now, at this watershed moment in human history, the 10 life-affirming traits that have been hardwired into the brains of women are urgently needed to help manage the complexities of our interconnected world.

Alexia Parks

WHO WE REALLY ARE

For more than 99.9% of human evolutionary history, our profession, both men and women, was that of the hunter-gatherer.

And just like the name implies, it was the hunter and gatherer of food. Food was everything. Food meant survival. Food was life itself.

We tend to forget about this, because today the total opposite is true. Not only is there an abundance of readily available food, the big problem today, in the developed world, is too much food, and obesity. Obesity is a modern day disease.

Throughout the evolutionary history of humans, there were many days when we went without food. There was never enough food. So, men would go out on long hunts in search of food. They would depend upon their testosterone driven denser muscles and bones to give them the strength and endurance they needed for the long journey.

Because of the long hunt, two of the major traits that became hardwired into the brains of men through evolutionary selection over millions of years, were: teamwork and one pointed concentration.

The Old Stone Age job of men required special skills. The men needed to work as a team, stay on the same wavelength, focus on the same goal, follow the deer, kill it, and then carry it home.

Due to the hardships our ancestors faced, and of significant importance, is the fact that over millions of years, the maximum lifespan of both men and women was only 25 years.

The stark reality of a 25-year life span resulted in a clear-cut division of labor between men and women.

As soon as women reached the age of puberty, they were either pregnant or nursing. The women, as the primary caregivers, were in charge of the survival of the children.

And this clear cut division of labor between men and women, the dichotomy that developed between the roles of men and women over millions of years, is **the KEY to the whole story that is unfolding here.**

Because women were either pregnant or nursing and could not participate with the men in the long grueling hunts, they developed a different set of evolutionary skills based around children, community and the hearth. The skills of women were life affirming and their success was measured in the survival of their children.

Just some of the traits which became hardwired in the brains of women, included the raising of children, the incredible social bonding skills between women in the community, their ability to both show emotions and understand the emotions of others in order to enhance communication, and a tremendous empathy for all of life.

These are just a few of the key traits hardwired into a woman's brain.

The chart in Part II contains all 10.

For now, the key message, which lies at the heart of the whole story is that these 10 special evolutionary traits, developed in women, just so happen to be the very traits that are needed for leadership in today's world.

They are hardwired and life affirming.

The Greatest Revolution In Human History

During the millions of years, known as the Old Stone Age, the average life span of men and women was a maximum of 25 years. They faced many dangers on a daily basis, and survival was always foremost on their mind.

Survival and the search for food were linked. In fact, food was survival itself. So, one could say, the mantra of this age was: **food, food, food**. And, if there had been a job listing posted during the Old Stone Age it would have read:

Wanted: One Hunter Gatherer.

While men went out in teams to hunt for food, sometimes on a run of 20 miles or longer, women, of necessity, stayed close to home at the hearth.

Pregnant or nursing, the job of the women was to ensure the survival of the children, and prepare the meal.

The tasks required by this division of labor became hardwired into their brains. Then, suddenly, in the "blink of an eye," after a long
sojourn in the wild lasting millions of years, the Agricultural Revolution began.

As recently as 10,000 years ago, in six "hot spots" around the world, the Agricultural Revolution began, and suddenly, everything changed.

And, where were those hot spots? They were in China, near Beijing; in India, in the Indus Valley; and in Iraq, in Mesopotamia – the fertile land between the Tigris and Euphrates Rivers. They also included "hot spots" in West Africa, Mexico, and the Andes.

With human settlement in mind, it could be said that the Agricultural Revolution was the greatest revolution in all of human history. It *could be said* that it was *infinitely* greater than the Russian Revolution, the French Revolution and the American Revolution.

Why was it greater than all of these? It was greater, because "overnight," we switched our occupation from the active, nomadic lifestyle of the hunter-gatherer to the more sedentary lifestyle of the farmer and city dweller.

THE 10 MAJOR CHANGES IN *HUMAN LIFESTYLE* FROM THE OLD STONE AGE TO THE AGRICULTURAL REVOLUTION © *Parks-Rauch Chart of Comparisons*		
The Old Stone Age		**The Agricultural Revolution**
100% Egalitarian & Functional	**Social Structure**	100% Hierarchical and Bureaucratic. Men vs Women
Active Nomadic Hunter-Gatherer	**Lifestyle**	Sedentary Farmer & City Dweller
Scarce	**Food Supply**	Abundant. The Domestication of Animals and Plants especially the cereal grains.
Around 100 (in small groups worldwide)	**Population Size**	Population Explosion
25 years maximum	**Life Span**	Approximately 75 years
Simple, with minimum material possessions.	**Complexity**	Very complex. Based on material possessions.
Lived off the land.	**Land**	Farming, private property, and irrigation rights.
None	**Legal System**	Complex
The Woman's Hearth	**Community Development**	The development of cities.
Very Simple	**Social Customs**	Very Complex

The Agricultural Revolution not only included massive cultivation of grain, specifically cereal grains, but also the domestication of many species of animals, including cows, pigs, sheep, and chickens.

For the first time in human history we did not have to go out the next day and look for food. We had as much food as we wanted. We became farmers, and sedentary village and city dwellers, instead of active, nomadic hunter-gatherers.

For the first time in human history, towns and cities arose. For the first time in human history, there was private property.

For the first time in human history, there were massive population explosions in areas where there was an abundance of food. For the first time in human history, giant bureaucracies and complex legal systems arose.

A tidal wave of change swept over the woman's hearth.

Men no longer went out to hunt. They stayed close to home. They built villages and cities.

As populations rapidly expanded, as overcrowding pushed greater numbers of people closer together, they became stratified into incredibly complex social structures and hierarchical systems.

Jails and court systems were built to manage the growing problems. To meet new demands, there was an explosion of material goods. There was also destruction of the environment.

The very mega-structure of rapidly expanding cities around world, and the complexity of rules and regulations to run them brought an abrupt end to the Old Stone Age.

I think you see the general picture. The stark contrast between the Old Stone Age and the Agricultural Revolution could not have been sharper.

Overnight everything changed. That is, almost everything changed.

The one thing that did not change, that remains true even today, were the evolutionary traits that were based on survival, and selectively hardwired into the brains of men and women over millions of years.

In general, it takes 100,000 years or longer to change our biology, our genetics.

While social customs and social mores are constantly evolving to reflect changing times, the hardwired traits of men and women take hundreds of thousands of years to change.

Because of this, the survival traits that were hardwired into humans in the Old Stone Age are still are present in men and women today.

Forged in a much simpler world where the division of labor was clearly defined, and based on the specific tasks that each of their jobs demanded, the brains of men and women were hardwired differently.

The chart that follows in Part II explains this more fully and includes all of the 10 major evolutionary traits of men and women. For now, a brief overview that touches on some of these traits will give you a general idea of these hardwired differences.

For the men, their hardwiring enabled them to focus on a single goal: to follow the deer, to hunt as a team, and to draw upon their testosterone driven strength and endurance for the long journey.

Of necessity, the evolutionary traits that were selected out in women included an ability to focus on many things at the same time, and to pay attention to everything in the local environment that supported her, including the flora and fauna.

Her ability to multi-task, and affirm everything that strengthened the health and well being of her children and her community, became part of her survival strategy.

This love of people and community has been hardwired into her brain. This was true for millions of years, and remains true today!

This fact alone is astounding to contemplate, and is so relevant today, that it bears repeating:

Women are hardwired with a love of people and community.

Even with the dramatic cultural changes brought to humankind by the Agricultural Revolution, nothing over the past 10,000 years has changed this evolutionary hardwiring in men and women.

The only thing that has changed has been the "learned behavior" of men and women based on the ever-changing nature of social and cultural customs.

These social and cultural customs have changed numerous times over the past 10,000 years, culture-by-culture, country-by-country, around the world.

From the perspective of evolutionary biology, which scientists and anthropologists now use as the basic model from which to study human evolution, there is a tremendous amount of hardwiring in the male and the female brain. Various estimates suggest that:

This hardwiring comprises 80% of the modern human brain.

If our brain is already 80% hardwired by evolutionary biology, what do we know about the remaining 20% percent?

Superimposed over this hardwiring is an outer layer of the brain called the cerebral cortex, or "the gray matter." The most highly developed part of the cerebral cortex is known as the frontal cortex, which does most of human thinking, including abstract thinking.

What is especially important to the anthropologists, brain scientists, and other professionals who study "learned behavior," is this frontal area: the frontal cortex.

The frontal cortex in humans determines a tremendous amount of learned behavior, or what is called "culture."

So, if the hardwired brain is looked at as *"hardware,"* then the newer part of the brain (the frontal cortex, the "plastic brain") which can adapt, learn new behaviors, and change as cultural rules and mores change, could be called the *"software"* of the brain.

The many different "software programs" used by the brain give it the quality referred to by modern science as **neuroplasticity**. Neuroplasticity refers to the "plastic" brain that can change itself, and is the hottest topic in brain function research today.

It is this malleable, "plastic" part of the brain which is shaped by 10,000 different cultures in 10,000 different ways.

Anthropologists have now classified over 10,000 separate cultures around the world. In addition, there are over 4,000 separate languages that have been classified, not counting dialects.

So, the ways in which a person "fits in" to their culture is learned behavior. Because 20% of the brain is malleable, it can

learn how to "fit in" to any culture, or respond to any
circumstance through upbringing, education and training.

For a reference point, consider how a dog is trained to be a
family pet. It can be trained for many different behaviors, and
respond to many different commands. **But, underneath its
learned behavior, is its evolutionary hardwiring**.

In humans, there are an infinite number of ways for the human
brain to be "domesticated;" that is, to learn how to adapt and fit
in to a culture.

**The neuroplastic brain, where learned behavior is shaped,
is only the "tip of the iceberg." The hardwired brain lies
just below the surface.**

To repeat, the hardwired brain makes up 80% of the human
brain.

The other 20% is where learned behavior takes place. And this can change as social customs and culture changes. It can also change through our interactions with people living in other cultures.

What this means, in terms of humans, is that men can learn "feminine behaviors" such as expressing emotions, tending to the home or hearth, and becoming primary caretakers of children.

However, while men can learn how to become primary caretakers of children, there is no society in the world where the men are the natural caretakers of children.

This is absolute. It is a *learned* behavior.

And conversely, women can learn "masculine behavior." They can learn how to be rough, tough soldiers. They can be trained to kill. They can join men on the hunt. They can become part of a team. They can also learn how to lower the tone of their voice, slow down their speech, and suppress their emotions.

In each case, this would be *learned behavior* as opposed to evolutionary hardwiring.

Said differently, the social customs of any culture are like the icing on a cake. The cake is the evolutionary hardwiring in both men and women. The icing on the cake would be the overlay of learning and culture in different parts of the world.

What lurks below the surface of social customs and culture is the hardwired brain. And the difference between the hardwired brain of a man and that of a woman makes all the difference in the world.

In fact, there is no other way to approach the human condition, and the future of life on Earth, but to understand the significance of the hardwired brain, and how it differs in men and women.

To see this big picture, one has to go beyond relationships, the workplace, politics, and the environment.

The big picture necessitates pulling from hard sciences such as medicine and evolutionary biology, and the soft sciences including sociology, psychology, and both cultural and physical anthropology.

The basis for our hardwired traits is the fact that for 99.9% of our life on Earth, we humans have lived out in the bush, out in

Nature. Our male and female brains were hardwired differently for the simple reason of survival.

Over those millions of years, the men and women who "got it right" were able to survive long enough to produce the next generation.

It's worth remembering that over most of human history, there were many days when food was scarce, and we went without food.

It is easy to forget that in the Old Stone Age, food was life itself, because today, just the opposite is true. Today, in most cities around the world, a person can have as much food as they want.

The abundance of food brought to us by the Agricultural Revolution, was the starting point for the whole drama that is unfolding in today's complex, volatile world.

So today, we have come full circle.

Over millions of years, because of the demands of reproduction, and the short life span of 25 years, women were relegated to the hearth.

However, as masters of the hearth, and because of their love of people and community, women develop many specialized talents and traits that insured the survival of their children and their community.

This is why these hardwired traits in women are the VERY TRAITS that make them the natural leaders for today's complex, volatile world.

And there is no right or wrong. Women are not better than men, they just hardwired differently. Necessity, as the cliché goes, is the mother of invention. And this hardwiring, based on necessity is, in a word, the basis of evolutionary biology.

This is how men and women were hardwired. Then, evolutionarily speaking, "in the blink of an eye," everything changed, as humans entered the Agricultural Revolution.

In terms of an evolutionary time frame, virtually overnight (only 10,000 years ago), the small groups of nomadic men and women around the world, numbering from 50 to 200 people, who traveled the land in search of food, were now stationary.

Once they became stationary and well fed, those small nomadic groups suddenly burgeoned into the massive populations of modern civilization.

Overnight, cities developed. Overnight, systems for "crowd control" developed. Massive bureaucracies were established. Religions multiplied. And legal systems for managing private property rights and agricultural rights were rapidly put into place.

With one-pointed concentration, men developed tools, machines, and technology, including ever more sophisticated weapons for waging war. These technologies and tools swept us forward at warp speed. Complexity skyrocketed.

Traveling at warp speed, we had to rapidly learn how to adapt to the ever-changing cultural demands placed upon us. We let ourselves become "domesticated." You could perhaps call it the "domestication" of the masculine and feminine mind.

Yet this is only learned behavior. The other 80% of the brain, the hardwired brain, is what breaks through the thin veneer of civilization, when push comes to shove.

For men and women, our hardwiring rises toward the surface when there is discord, or disputation. It reveals itself when there is fear, or a threat, or when "the other" comes into view.

And its important to remind ourselves that it takes hundreds of thousands of years for evolution to select out these traits and hardwire them into humans. And the new information is this:

That the very traits that were selected out over that time frame in women, by the pressures and necessity of survival, are the very traits that could save the world today.

The chart and discussion that follows in Part II makes the reason for this very, very clear.

PART II

Alexia Parks

Hardwired to Save the World

In the chart that follows, we intentionally summarized huge amounts of data from major fields that all converge on the same thesis and that is:

That the very traits that were hardwired and selected out by Mother Nature for women, are ironically the very traits that are needed to save the world today.

And, as stated, there is no right or wrong. In evolutionary biology, necessity is the Mother of Invention. That is how evolutionary biology works.

In this case, Mother Nature, through evolutionary biology, has selected out certain traits for human survival itself. And the traits hardwired in women and men apply to everything that is happening in the world today, including relationships between men and women.

However, the issue humans face today, is survival on a larger scale, a global scale. Our interconnected relationships and alliances now include the whole world and its 10,000 different cultures.

The skills of men have brought us this far, over millions of years, and their major traits are summarized in the chart.

The chart could also be called: *"The Chart of Opposites."*

It shows why the leadership traits that are needed to manage the complexities of today's world require a woman's brain.

The 10 Traits of A Great World Leader

Take a look at the following list and see if you agree with me that these leadership traits are what the world needs now in a great leader.

1. Community building skills
2. Social bonding that includes diverse cultures
3. The ability to freely express emotions, as well as understand and respond to the emotional needs of others.
4. Empathy for others.
5. The ability to easily display affections.
6. A love of people and community
7. Multi-tasking skills at many levels, simultaneously
8. Acute awareness of, and a love of, the environment.
9. Success at balancing many different competing factors.
10. Great diplomatic, negotiating, and problem-solving skills. Skilled at decision-making, with the ability to befriend adversaries and create win-win situations.

	THE 10 MAJOR TRAITS HARDWIRED IN MEN & WOMEN © Parks-Rauch Chart of Hardwired Traits	
Male Traits	**Hardwired**	**Female Traits**
Teamwork	**Social Mind**	Social Networking
Testosterone Driven. Aggressive. Strength & Endurance. Muscle and Bone Density	**Hormones**	Estrogen, Oxytocin, Bonding. Stored fat that converts to milk when nursing.
Suppresses emotions.	**Emotions**	Readily Displays Emotions; Easily reads the emotions of others.
Low Levels of Empathy	**Empathy**	Highly Empathetic
Harder for men to touch.	**Touch**	Displays touch and affection easily
Love of machines, tools & technology.	**Primary Love**	Love of people and community
Focused Concentration	**Goal Setting**	Multi-Tasking
Lower	**Fine Point Discrimination**	Higher
Lower	**Balancing Many Factors Simultaneously**	Higher
Fight or Flight	**Facing Danger**	Tend & Befriend

1 THE SOCIAL MIND

The social mind of men is based on teamwork.

To be on a team requires that everyone on that team be tuned into the same "radio station," that is, the same wavelength. The team must share a common language that is mutually understandable and precise. Everyone on the team must stay focused on a common goal.

With this in mind, remember that the work of the men of the Old Stone Age was that of the hunter-gatherer, and they hunted as a team. Their common goal, on a daily basis, was to stay focused on food: to follow the food, to hunt down the deer, then kill it and carry it back to the village.

This long distance hunt that covered many miles, and could last for several days, required strength, stamina, and aggression by the men.

It also required long periods of social isolation, and an ever-present risk of injury, pain and suffering.

In short, it required that men learn to suppress their emotions for the greater good of the team. It also required that they kill without empathy, because they knew that food was survival itself.

This constellation of characteristics, selected out over millions of years by evolutionary biology, paints a picture of the condition of men that required their teamwork. These traits became hardwired, and shaped the social mind of men.

The social mind of women is based on social networking.

In contrast to men, women who have evolved over millions of years in community and at the hearth, developed a social mind that was able to freely express emotions and feel empathy for those who suffer or who have unmet needs.

Women, in other words, are much better at social communication and community bonding, than men.

The focus of women is on sustaining life. They are life affirming and interested in the well being of others.

Over millennia, the skills associated with social networking, including a woman's ability to interact with, and balance out the diverse interests of others became hardwired in her brain.

This fact, affirmed by research in evolutionary biology, is important to emphasize and restate.

Women are much better at communicating their emotions than men. They are hardwired to be empathetic and easily read other people's emotions, both verbal and non-verbal.

And part of the hardwiring of women is for the greater good of the community. Women are constantly bonding on every level for the greater good of the community, and especially for the benefit of the children.

Today we know that a lot of communication is based on emotional intelligence. It has been selected out, that is, hardwired, because it is the glue that bonds together the entire community for the purpose of raising children.

What women have known for millions of years, that is still true today is this: "It takes a village to raise a child."

While the community of the Old Stone Age has now become a "community of nations", a large part of the behavior of both men and women today, is still based on our evolutionary hardwiring.

Today, however, the complexity of various cultures around the world, brought to us by the Agricultural Revolution, overshadows the hardwiring.

The cultural overlay is the icing on the cake, so to speak. The hardwired "cake," prepared for humankind, was baked over hundreds of thousands of years.

The icing, or complex social and cultural customs, along with cultural conditioning, was only added recently.

Today, if anyone takes a course in cultural anthropology, they will learn that there are over 100 groups that are marginal around the world that still live in the Old Stone Age. So by studying those 100 groups around the world, anthropologists are really looking at humans before we made the transition into the Agricultural Revolution.

Of the 100 groups, the most famous group, which has been studied the most, are SAN Bushmen of the Kalahari Desert of South Africa.

2   HORMONES

Men & Testosterone.

When a baby is born, it is held up, and the first question that is usually asked is: Is it a boy or girl? This is called the **primary** sexual characteristic, and it is very obvious.

However, the major difference between boys and girls in adolescence is the hormone Testosterone. Testosterone is what makes little boys, boys.

What are some of those **secondary** sexual characteristics of Testosterone in boys and men? They include denser muscles, denser bones, more risk-taking behavior, more aggressive behavior than women, and the ability to suppress emotions.

In short, Testosterone is the perfect hormone for the rigor and endurance demanded in a long distant hunt by a team of men.

The hormone Testosterone, in fact, actually changes the structure, or hardwiring, of the male brain to be more aggressive and more risk-taking.

Women and Estrogen

By contrast, what makes little girls, girls, is the hormone Estrogen. And what are some of the **secondary** characteristics of Estrogen? It isn't dense muscles and bone. Instead it is a much greater percentage of body fat both in the hip area, and the women's breasts.

Why does Estrogen drive so much more body fat in women than in men?

The function of body fat in women, which developed over
hundreds of thousands of years, was to ensure the survival of
the nursing baby. The body fat in women was carried as stored
calories for the baby, when there wasn't enough food for the
woman to eat.

This stored fat was converted into breast milk for the nursing
baby. The hormone, Estrogen, that facilitates this conversion,
was hardwired into a woman's hormonal system by Mother
Nature. It acted like an insurance policy to make sure that
there would be enough food for the baby, when food was
scarce.

So, women who have muscles and bones that are not as dense
as men, have instead, a much higher percentage of body fat. In
medical anthropology, for example, the large buttocks of

women of childbearing age, even in petite women, is referred to as steatopygia.

Steatopygia means the storage of calories in the buttocks area, because those calories of fat can be translated into milk for the baby during lean times.

Along with a higher percentage of body fat, the hormone Estrogen in women also means that they will have higher voices, and no facial hair.

And, perhaps the most important characteristic, in light of the subject of this book is this: **Due to the lack of the Testosterone hormone, women are less aggressive and better at social bonding than men.**

Women and Oxytocin

The hormone Oxytocin is basically known as the bonding hormone. The strongest bond in humans is the mother-baby bond. The maternal bond is cemented by the hormone Oxytocin.

Oxytocin is released from the master gland, the pituitary gland in the mother's brain, as soon as a baby suckles. A neuronal reflex in her brain will release it. The first time the baby goes for the breast milk, the hormone Oxytocin is released for the bonding of the baby with the mother.

This is hardwired in women. Through Oxytocin, women are chemically bonded with their children, and by extension, with their family and their community.

For men, in general, bonding with their children is more of a learned behavior, through upbringing, education, parenting, and social customs.

The significance of this fact and other hardwired differences between men and women cannot be emphasized enough.

Why?

These hardwired differences relate to every single human being on the planet. They show up in the way we respond to relationships, the workplace, to politics, to economics, to the environment, to raising children, to adolescents, to marriage, and about 100 other major topics.

In short, the attributes that are hardwired by evolutionary biology in humans relate to every single human endeavor in the world today.

> **As mentioned earlier, in the chart of traits, we intentionally summarized huge amounts of data from major fields that all converge on the same thesis. And this is that *the very traits* that were hardwired and selected out by Mother Nature for women *are, ironically,* the very traits that are needed today to save the world.**

There is no right or wrong. The traits of men and women were selected, by necessity, for survival itself; and the skills of men have brought us this far, over millions of years.

Now, the issue is survival on a larger scale, and includes the whole world.

So, if there truly is a need to "Save the World," there needs to be a quantum shift toward *women in leadership roles* at all levels of society.

The natural leadership skills of women, hardwired into their brain for more than 100,000 years, are the very skills needed to lead us forward through the complexities of today's volatile world.

3 EMOTIONS

Because women were relegated to the hearth, and childrearing for most of human history, a women's emotional brain is bigger and better developed, than a man's emotional brain. It is also known as the limbic system.

The reason for its larger size in women is due to evolutionary biology. For over 99.9% of human history, the job of women was to bond, not only with their children, and the animals that lived with them, but to also bond and interact with other women.

This emotional bonding helped insure a social network of support from other women in the community.

In the Old Stone Age, the HEART of the women's hearth was the group of socially connected women, their children, their animals, and the simple tools they used for cooking and meal preparation.

This natural form of emotional communication ensured their survival. Today it is referred to as emotional intelligence and is a key leadership skill.

Women excel at emotional intelligence. A women is not only better at showing emotions, but is also better at reading the emotions of others, both verbal and non-verbal.

Remember that old cliché, "a woman's intuition"? This refers to her ability to read the emotions of others. It is a key benefit gained from the woman's larger emotional brain. Her brain is hardwired to be more expressive.

By contrast, men are hardwired with a smaller emotional brain. This smaller emotional brain was selected out through evolutionary biology for the ability of men to *suppress* their emotions. The ability to suppress emotions is not a learned behavior in men; it is hardwired.

To emphasize this point: over millions of years, driven by the incredible pressure of the long distance hunt, those men who were able to suppress their emotions became valued members of the hunting team.

The physically demanding tasks of the hunt, required men who were able to suppress their emotions when injured, or in pain.

Evolution selected out men who could suppress their fear when attacked by an animal, or when they were participating in a kill.

Men hunting together in a team knew that if they showed any emotions, or any feelings at all, this display of emotions would be perceived as a sign of weakness.

For the success of the team, there could be no weak link to distract them, or slow them down on their long distance hunt. The demands of their job meant that they could not be distracted by pain, suffering, or fear.

Because of the hardwired suppression of emotions in men, the way they communicate is a lot more intellectual, a lot more left brain and unemotional.

Men learned to suppress any stirrings of the emotional brain for the greater good of the team while out on the hunt, and to show strength for the kill.

By contrast, women learned to express their emotions for the greater good of their social network, for community bonding, and for child rearing. Over time, their ability to freely express their emotions became hardwired.

4   **EMPATHY**

The emotional brain of women has been hardwired to be able to read the emotions of her children, the animals around the hearth, and to read the emotions of other people on both a verbal and non-verbal level.

She has to be able to quickly understand the emotional needs of those who are not able to fully communicate them.

Another name for this trait is empathy.

The low empathy of men would be part of the same constellation of traits that gave them the ability to suppress emotions for the long distance hunt, the ability to dispassionately kill animals, and even, in warfare, to kill other humans.

In general, when a man sees someone who is sad, it doesn't affect him the same way as a woman, because he is hardwired to suppress his emotions. He is part of a team. He doesn't want to spend time trying to understand or empathize with the unstated needs of his teammates.

With women, it's just the opposite.

5   TOUCH

Another characteristic of the emotional brain of women is their constant touching and nurturing of children, friends and community. This has been hardwired for social bonding, and helps unite the community.

It is worth noting here that Jane Goodall's chimps, who share 99.5% of our DNA, in the exact same sequence, will spend the whole day constantly grooming, and touching each other, for the greater good of social bonding in the community.

Touching, hugging, holding hands, and dancing as a group, all elevate the social bonding of a community.

So, in addition to the emotional brain, women also have a much greater ability to show affection by way of touch.

Again, by contrast, men have been hardwired through the "loneliness of the long distance hunt," to suppress emotions, empathy, and touch. When men do touch, it is very superficial and ritualistic. In western cultures, a strong handshake between men will suffice.

In addition, there is a phenomenon called homophobia, the fear or hatred of homosexuals. This fear reinforces the pre-existing, hardwired taboo of touch in men, and makes casual physical contact with each other more difficult.

6   PRIMARY LOVE

Men love their motorcycles. Men love their cars. Men who go to war, have been known to paint symbolic images of women on their weapons, and give them a women's name.

Men are known for their love of machines, tools and technology.

It could be said that the primary love of men is inanimate, dead objects: tool making, tools, and technology.

By contrast, in women, it's a primary love of people and community.

And scientifically speaking, this is true. Researchers at Cambridge and the University College of London's School of

Economics have done extensive research in this area on both women and men.

The term these researchers use to describe a man's love of tools, technology and tool-making, that is hardwired by evolutionary biology into their brain is: "systematic thinkers."

A primary love is also hardwired into the mental ("mentalistic") sphere of women, but in stark contrast to the hardwiring of men, these research studies confirm that women have a profound love of people and community.

From the Old Stone Age up to modern times, men have been, and continue to be systematic thinkers. Their orientation is toward dead, inanimate objects meaning that they love machines, technology and tools. This primary love of men is their love of technology, and a love of trying to figure out how things work.

And for this, we owe a debt of gratitude to men. Their goal-setting skills and teamwork with regard to technology and tools have brought us this far.

The leadership of men has brought us to where we are today, and we have prospered. Now, the times have changed.

Different times require different solutions. The challenges that lie ahead for the world necessitate the use of a different set of skills. They demand a shift of focus.

Some would say that the world is at a tipping point, a watershed moment.

The complexity of today's world demands that more attention be paid to all life on Earth. It demands that we focus on solutions that are people oriented, community oriented, life sustaining, and life affirming.

Could it be that we as a human species have come full circle, and that today, we are at the same crisis point that humankind faced in the Old Stone Age? Survival itself?

Do women feel an intuitive need to "Save the World?" Could now be the time for women to step into leadership roles and lead the way forward?

Women have been hardwired, for more than 100,000 years for this life sustaining, life-affirming role.

Today, women engaged in leadership at all levels, in all cultures, could instantly shift the conversations, the focus, and the direction of policy toward their primary love.

I have described a way for women to accomplish this shift "overnight," in *The Luck of the Irish* at the end of this book.

Alexia Parks

7   GOAL SETTING

In looking at the trait of goal setting, let's focus on men first,

and their skill of one-pointed, focused concentration.

Remember that we spoke earlier about the evolutionary

pressure on men to become part of a long distance

testosterone-driven team?

The goal for each man, and collectively as a team, was a simple

one. They had to bring back food to the women and children,

which sustained life itself. There was no margin of error.

The main characteristic that men developed in a team, that became hardwired in their brain, was incredible focus and concentration.

They became skilled at cybernetic goal setting, focusing with one pointed concentration on their goal, just like a cruise missile or drone will zig and zag until it converges on the target.

So men, compared to women, do not like distractions.

Men function best when there is a single focus, a clear-cut, affirmative goal, and the use of a common language to keep them on the same wavelength.

This intense focus is also seen in the traditional, male dominated corporate world, as employees are trained to work in teams and focus on achieving a single goal. It also shows up in extreme conditions such as war, and is reinforced through the training of soldiers and military personnel around the world.

By contrast, the hardwired traits of women noted here are almost diametrically opposite to those of men. And it is easy to see why those traits are urgently needed in leadership roles today to help manage our complex, volatile world.

Over human history, because of the very nature of the hearth, women had to balance out many competing demands at the same time. She had to focus on the demands of the children, the animals, the meal preparation and cooking, the gathering of local herbs and plants, along with many other tasks.

Today this is roughly synonymous with what we call multi-tasking. Men are hardwired to have one goal, one objective. **Women are hardwired to be able to balance many goals simultaneously.**

And the startling fact is this. Brain studies show that the connection between the two brain hemispheres, left and right, is much more highly developed in women.

This more highly developed connection, called "The Bridge of Consciousness," or Corpus Callosum, has been enhanced in a woman's brain for multi-tasking and balancing out many factors.

8 FINE POINT DISCRIMINATION

Because of the local food gathering ability of women of the Old Stone Age, a woman's brain is hardwired for fine point discrimination.

Fine point discrimination refers to a woman's hardwired ability to be able to dissect out the various species of plants, seeds, herbs, and colors, around the hearth, or home.

A woman can see *both* the forest AND the trees.

Interestingly, the hottest new theory in cultural anthropology is that the origin of the Agricultural Revolution belongs to seed gathering women, who discovered that seeds could also be planted, and ultimately, harvested.

Again, it is worth remembering that in hunter-gatherer times, because women were either pregnant or nursing, they were relegated to the hearth. They could not leave nursing, and the children behind in order to hunt with the men. So, in addition, to raising children and animals, a great amount of their time was spent becoming experts of the local flora and fauna.

Because of this role in gathering food from around the hearth, women's brains are much better at determining which plants are edible and which are weeds; which herbs are medicinal and beneficial as botanicals. This trait is hardwired.

Men, on the other hand, are just the opposite. Because their job was to hunt for food, they have been hardwired for a total focus on the target. And the target, of course, was the object of the hunt.

So women, in a multi-sensory environment, are much better at detecting subtleties of colors, shapes, and textures.

Men are much better at cybernetic goal setting and keeping everyone focused on achieving a common goal.

9 BALANCING MANY FACTORS AT ONCE

Because of the relegation of women to the hearth, where many things were occurring at many levels, simultaneously, one of the major evolutionary traits hardwired in women is their ability to balance out many competing factors, in real time.

The woman's brain has been neurologically wired to balance out everything and prioritize at the same time.

So, for example, women were able to balance out the attention of the children, the family, the needs of the animals, the bonding with other women in the community, and at the same time, attend to the necessities of the hearth in terms of food

preparation, and gathering local seeds, herbs and plants.

By contrast, men did not need to learn how to balance out many things at the same time. With one pointed focus, everything else was viewed as a distraction.

Men learned to be successful at ignoring anything that

distracted from the goal. Their brain became hardwired to

focus on the cybernetic goal they had selected, and to mentally

discard any extraneous factors. As mentioned earlier, these

factors might include the distractions of pain, suffering,

emotions, hunger, or thirst that they or others might feel, while

engaged in a long distance hunt.

10   FACING DANGER

We've all heard of the **"flight or fight"** response of men when faced with danger. Men, supported by testosterone, strong muscles and dense bones, will quickly assess the situation and then make a quick calculation. They will either stay to fight, and hopefully win, or run away from the situation. They will slay the saber tooth tiger, or run from it. They will fire the weapon, push the button, or wait.

Women, on the other hand, will **"tend and befriend."** They will move toward danger, not away from it. What is the reason for this, and *why* is it hardwired in the brain of women to befriend danger?

Through extensive research, anthropologists believe that because women of the Old Stone Age were either pregnant or nursing, and had children and animals around her, she could *not* fight or run away in an instant, like men.

This inability to run away shaped an opposite response in women. Therefore, with any potential danger, women would tend to negotiate, to befriend, and to try to work things out.

In short, when a woman is confronted with danger, all of her hardwired social skills are brought to bear on the situation.

This is not learned behavior. This is the hardwired behavior of women selected out over hundreds of thousands of years of living out in the wild, out in Mother Nature.

WHAT THE WORLD NEEDS NOW

Biology Drives Everything.

Everything is, basically, biologically driven. Eighty percent of

our brain is hardwired and lies just below the surface of

learned behavior. It is who we really are.

Today, the skills that are needed in leadership roles at all levels

of society are those that are able to multi-task, in real time. To

be able to balance out many competing interests, in real time.

.

It is not just one goal, one target, one direction, and endless

wars to win. It's no longer about winners and losers. And it's all

happening simultaneously.

In this new emerging world the question is: How can we let everyone win? How can we manage this complexity so that everyone benefits?

The skill sets that are needed to manage this level of complexity in today's volatile world belong to women.

A women's leadership skills were forged at the hearth over millions of years.

The original children around her hearth are now the children of the world. We now live in a "global village."

The animals she tended and the local plants she gathered around the hearth have now become the animals and ecology of the world. Our world is interconnected.

A woman's community in the Old Stone Age has now become a community of nations. Our needs are intertwined.

Today, the very qualities that were hardwired into a woman's brain and hormones around the hearth are now the very qualities needed to manage the complexities of our socially-networked, volatile world.

Why would women make the best leaders of today's world?

- Because a woman's brain is hardwired to be life affirming

- A women's brain is able to express emotions

- A woman's brain intuits the healing power of touch

- Her brain has fine point discrimination. It can see the forest AND the trees at the same time.

- The focus of women, as leaders, would shift toward people and community. The filter that women in leadership would add to decision-making and policy-making would be this:

Does (this action)(this technology)(this proposal) protect, sustain, and affirm life? Is it beneficial to all?

Today, the original hearth of women has become the hearth of the world. The Earth is now her home.

Now is the time for women to lead the way forward.

THE LUCK OF THE IRISH

There was a time in American history when the potato famine in Ireland prompted a mass immigration of the Irish to America.

In the mid 1800's, the Irish arrived by the millions on our eastern shores, and moved into large cities such as New York City and Boston. However, their numbers were so vast, that there was an immediate backlash.

Their overwhelming numbers threatened the jobs of those who had arrived before them. So warning signs were posted in storefront windows and wherever "help wanted" notices were placed: "IRISH need not apply."

They threatened the status quo, and the economic stability of those who already had jobs.

So what did the Irish do? *They picked leaders from among their ranks and then voted them into office.*

Once in political office, the Irish politicians quickly identified jobs for the Irish as policemen and fire fighters. It didn't take long before the prejudice against the Irish was gone. They were no longer suppressed. Today, we celebrate the Irish, with a St Patrick's Day Parade.

How does the luck of the Irish apply to women?

It wasn't luck. It was numbers. Think of the Kennedy clan. Irish men were able to garner enough votes to propel them into politics.

Today, women comprise 50% of the world's population, yet in the G8 countries they comprise, on average, only 16% of its leaders. **By using the power of their vote, they can select, and vote women into leadership positions "overnight."**

Overnight, they can save the world!

THE 10 TRAITS OF A GREAT WORLD LEADER
© *Parks--Rauch Leadership Chart*

Do You Have the Skills of a Great Leader?

	TRAIT *10 = Highly Skilled*	1	2	3	4	5	6	7	8	9	10	SCORE
1	Social Networking											
2	Bonding											
3	Expressive											
4	Empathetic											
5	Nurturing											
6	Love of People											
7	Multi-Tasking											
8	Detects Subtleties											
9	Balance & Prioritize											
10	Tend & Befriend											
Your Score												

ORDER FORM

Special Offer. Receive a **15% discount** when you buy 5 books or more.

Bulk Purchase Discount. Receive **40% discount** for orders of 100 – 1,000 or more books. To order, please call publisher.

PHONE	**303-443-3697**
EMAIL	alexiaparks@gmail.com
WEBSITE	http://theeducationexchange.org
MAIL	The Education Exchange Network
	973 5th Street, Boulder, CO 80302

Quantity		Code	Price
1	**HARDWIRED**		19.95
5	FIVE Pack	FAM	85.00
100+	Bulk Purchase	CALL	40%

Your Name_____

Address_____

City_____State_____Zip_____

Credit Card #_____

Name on Card:_____

Made in the USA
Charleston, SC
21 March 2012